EXtreme Animals

The Smallest Animals

by Megan Cooley Peterson

Consulting Editor: Gail Saunders-Smith, PhD

Consultant: Tanya Dewey, PhD
University of Michigan Museum of Zoology

CAPSTONE PRESS
a capstone imprint

Pebble Plus is published by Capstone Press,
1710 Roe Crest Drive, North Mankato, Minnesota 56003.
www.capstonepub.com

Library of Congress Cataloging-in-Publication Data
Peterson, Megan Cooley.
  The smallest animals / by Megan Cooley Peterson.
      p. cm.—(Pebble plus. Extreme animals)
  Includes bibliographical references and index.
  Summary: "Simple text and photographs present the world's smallest animals"—Provided by publisher.
  ISBN 978-1-4296-7600-7 (library binding)
  ISBN 978-1-4296-7903-9 (paperback)
  1. Body size—Juvenile literature. 2. Animals—Juvenile literature. I. Title. II. Series.
QL799.3.P48 2012
590—dc23   2011026932

Editorial Credits
Katy Kudela, editor; Heidi Thompson, set designer; Alison Thiele, book designer; Svetlana Zhurkin, media researcher;
    Kathy McColley, production specialist

Photo Credits
Alamy: Juniors Bildarchiv, 8–9, Lee Dalton, 7, Nigel Cattlin, 20–21; Ardea: Steve Downer, 10–11; Corbis: dpa/Miguel
Vences, 15, epa/S. Blair Hedges, 13, Reuters/Handout, 17; Newscom: WENN/ZOB/JP5, 1; Photo Researchers:
Dr. Harold Rose, 18–19, Dr. Merlin D. Tuttle, cover; Shutterstock: Karel Gallas, 5

Note to Parents and Teachers

The Extreme Animals series supports national science standards related to life science.
This book describes and illustrates small animals. The images support early readers in
understanding the text. The repetition of words and phrases helps early readers learn new
words. This book also introduces early readers to subject-specific vocabulary words, which are
defined in the Glossary section. Early readers may need assistance to read some words and to
use the Table of Contents, Glossary, Read More, Internet Sites, and Index sections of the book.

Printed in the United States of America in North Mankato, Minnesota.
102011   006405CGS12

Table of Contents

Small

They are teensy! They are puny!

They are hard to find!

These animals aren't just small.

Their small size is EXTREME.

Swish! A pygmy marmoset

dashes through rain forest trees.

Thick leaves hide these monkeys

from snakes, eagles, and hawks.

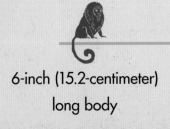

6-inch (15.2-centimeter)

long body

Bee hummingbirds weigh less than a penny. The world's smallest birds easily hover near flowers to drink nectar. They flap their wings 80 times per second.

2.25 inches
(5.7 cm) long

Jerboas live in the deserts
of Asia, Europe, and Africa.
Large back legs make these
rodents fast jumpers. They hop
into burrows to stay safe.

1.4–6-inch
(3.6–15.2-cm) long body

Smaller

Swoosh! A Kitti's hog-nosed bat swoops through the night sky. Its body is only the size of a large bumblebee. But its wingspan is 6 inches (15.2 cm).

1.18-inch (3-cm)
long body

Dwarf geckos hide under leaves

on the rain forest floor.

These tiny lizards are hard to find.

But if caught they can drop

their tails to get away.

0.62-inch (1.6-cm)

long body

The Monte Iberia frog from Cuba

can fit on a person's fingernail!

But this frog is no pushover.

Its poisonous skin makes a

deadly meal for predators.

0.39 inches
(1 cm) long

Smallest

Stout infantfish live in Australia's Great Barrier Reef. They have tiny, see-through bodies. Predators have trouble finding them.

0.28 inch
(7 millimeters) long

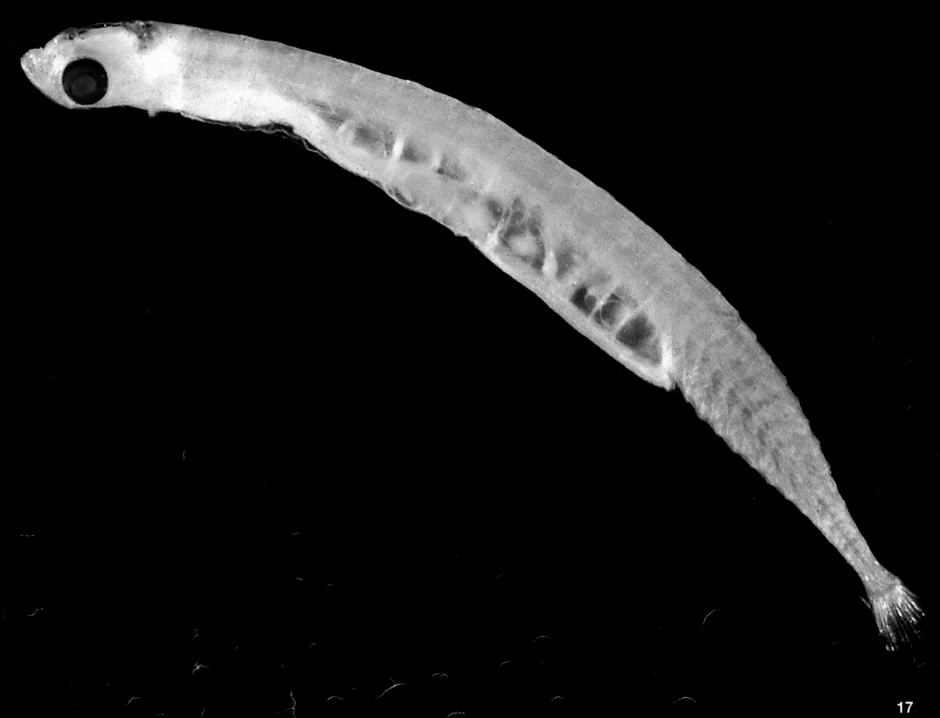

Female fairyfly wasps lay eggs
inside the eggs of other insects.
The larvae feed on the eggs.
Then the larvae chew
their way out.

up to 0.16 inch
(4 mm) long

Chomp! Dust mites eat dead
skin cells. Millions of mites
can live in one house.
You'll need a microscope
to see them!

less than 0.02 inch
(0.5 mm) long

21

Glossary

burrow—a tunnel or hole in the ground made or used by an animal

extreme—very great

hover—to remain in one place in the air

larva—an insect at the stage of development between an egg and an adult

microscope—a tool that makes very small things look large enough to be seen

nectar—a sweet liquid found in many flowers

poisonous—able to harm or kill with poison or venom

predator—an animal that hunts other animals for food

rodent—a mammal with long front teeth used for gnawing

wingspan—the distance between the tips of a pair of wings when fully open

Read More

Kenney, Karen Latchana. *Tiny Animals.* Our Animal World. Mankato, Minn.: Amicus, 2011.

Mitchell, Susan K. *Biggest vs. Smallest Creepy, Crawly Creatures.* Biggest vs. Smallest Animals. Berkeley Heights, N.J.: Bailey Books/Enslow Publishers, 2011.

Murray, Julie. *Smallest Animals.* That's Wild!: A Look at Animals. Edina, Minn.: ABDO Pub., 2010.

Internet Sites

FactHound offers a safe, fun way to find Internet sites related to this book. All of the sites on FactHound have been researched by our staff.

Here's all you do:

Visit *www.facthound.com*

Type in this code: 9781429676007

Super-cool stuff! Check out projects, games and lots more at
www.capstonekids.com

23

Index

Word Count: 238
Grade: 1
Early-Intervention Level: 22